GENERAL CATALOG SHOWING
COLORED ENGRAVINGS
OF

The "Pendleton" Line

MANUFACTURED BY THE

Pendleton Woolen Mills
Pendleton, Oregon

A reprint in its entirety of the first significant catalog produced by Pendleton Woolen Mills for the sale of its "Indian design" bed blankets, robes, steamer rugs, bath robes, couch covers, tapestries and shawls.

Avanyu Publishing Inc.

New Material ©1987
AVANYU PUBLISHING, Inc.
P.O. Box 27134
Albuquerque, New Mexico 87125

Library of Congress Card Catalog Number
87-12613

ISBN 0-936755-24-5

The prices quoted in this catalog are not binding on Pendleton Woolen Mills.

This work has been produced with the consent, permission, approval and cooperation of the Pendleton Woolen Mills, Inc. Portland, Oregon 97207

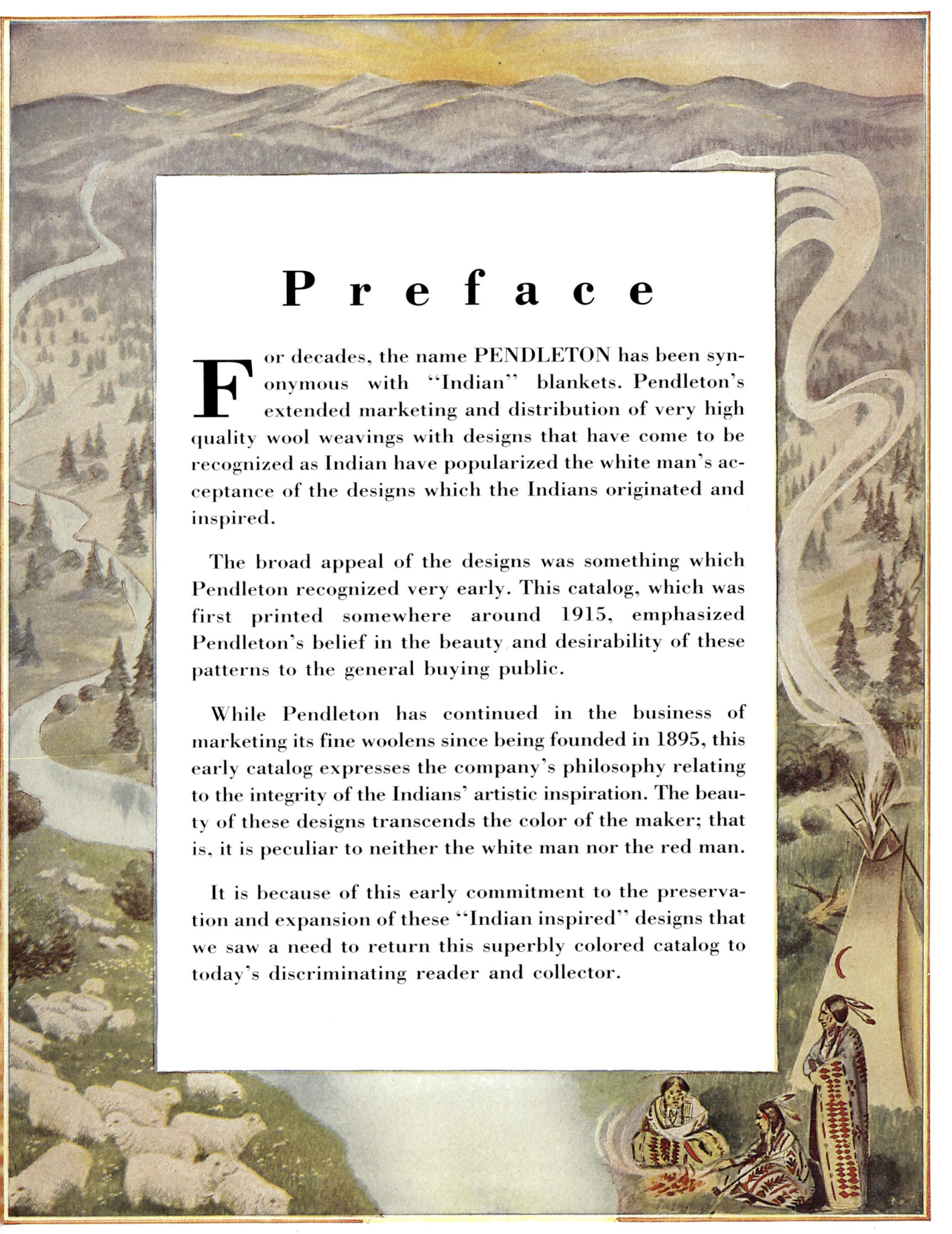

Preface

For decades, the name PENDLETON has been synonymous with "Indian" blankets. Pendleton's extended marketing and distribution of very high quality wool weavings with designs that have come to be recognized as Indian have popularized the white man's acceptance of the designs which the Indians originated and inspired.

The broad appeal of the designs was something which Pendleton recognized very early. This catalog, which was first printed somewhere around 1915, emphasized Pendleton's belief in the beauty and desirability of these patterns to the general buying public.

While Pendleton has continued in the business of marketing its fine woolens since being founded in 1895, this early catalog expresses the company's philosophy relating to the integrity of the Indians' artistic inspiration. The beauty of these designs transcends the color of the maker; that is, it is peculiar to neither the white man nor the red man.

It is because of this early commitment to the preservation and expansion of these "Indian inspired" designs that we saw a need to return this superbly colored catalog to today's discriminating reader and collector.

Please accept this volume as an expression of gratitude to the Pendleton Woolen Mills, Inc. for its influence in sharing the beauty of the Indians' designs with so many people for so many years.

Our special thanks go out to Mr. E. A. Pedley of the Pendleton Woolen Mills, Inc., for all his assistance in providing background information on the catalog and to Ernie Bulow of Buffalo Medicine Books, Gallup, New Mexico, for finding the original copy of the catalog from which this reprint is reproduced and finally to Bob and Marianne Kapoun of The Shop of the Rainbow Man in Santa Fe, New Mexico for their assistance and cooperation in the reprinting of this catalog.

J. Brent Ricks   Alexander E. Anthony Jr.

Avanyu Publishing, Inc.
PO Box 27134
Albuquerque, NM 87125

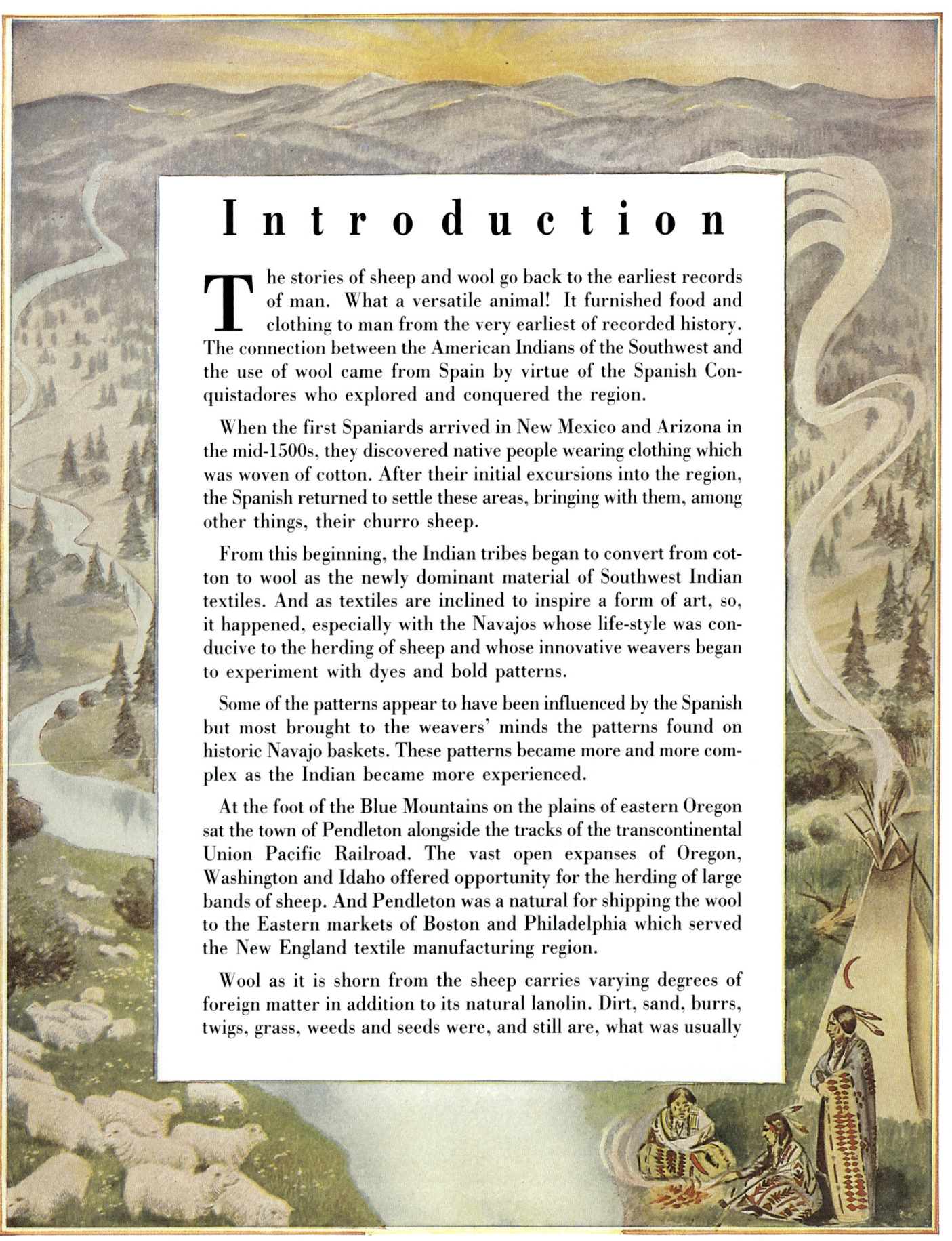

Introduction

The stories of sheep and wool go back to the earliest records of man. What a versatile animal! It furnished food and clothing to man from the very earliest of recorded history. The connection between the American Indians of the Southwest and the use of wool came from Spain by virtue of the Spanish Conquistadores who explored and conquered the region.

When the first Spaniards arrived in New Mexico and Arizona in the mid-1500s, they discovered native people wearing clothing which was woven of cotton. After their initial excursions into the region, the Spanish returned to settle these areas, bringing with them, among other things, their churro sheep.

From this beginning, the Indian tribes began to convert from cotton to wool as the newly dominant material of Southwest Indian textiles. And as textiles are inclined to inspire a form of art, so, it happened, especially with the Navajos whose life-style was conducive to the herding of sheep and whose innovative weavers began to experiment with dyes and bold patterns.

Some of the patterns appear to have been influenced by the Spanish but most brought to the weavers' minds the patterns found on historic Navajo baskets. These patterns became more and more complex as the Indian became more experienced.

At the foot of the Blue Mountains on the plains of eastern Oregon sat the town of Pendleton alongside the tracks of the transcontinental Union Pacific Railroad. The vast open expanses of Oregon, Washington and Idaho offered opportunity for the herding of large bands of sheep. And Pendleton was a natural for shipping the wool to the Eastern markets of Boston and Philadelphia which served the New England textile manufacturing region.

Wool as it is shorn from the sheep carries varying degrees of foreign matter in addition to its natural lanolin. Dirt, sand, burrs, twigs, grass, weeds and seeds were, and still are, what was usually found in freshly shorn wool. This foreign matter, plus the lanolin, can run as much as 60% of the total weight of raw wool. Then two fellows from the Boston market had the idea of installing a wool scouring mill at Pendleton so that just the clean wool would be shipped. There was no sense to paying freight on the dirt, sand and burrs! It was a good idea but the railroad had its own answer. The Union Pacific put in a new rate on the cleaned wool which more than offset the savings anticipated by the wool scouring people. After the wool scouring enterprise was established about 1892, the owners of the scouring mill brought in textile manufacturing equipment and the Pendleton Woolen Mills was started in 1895.

This time period saw the completion of and initiation into business of many small woolen mills in western Oregon to handle the wool produced in the area. The product most easily produced by these smaller mills was the blanket. The Pendleton mill also made blankets. But Pendleton's blankets were different. Pendleton had employed as a textile designer a man named Joe Rounsley who was a graduate of the highly acclaimed Philadelphia Textile School.

In 1909, the Bishop family bought the Pendleton Woolen Mills, built a new building, improved the machinery, and entered into the growing competition for business. Situated as a neighbor to the Nez Perce Indian Nation, and with Clarence and Roy Bishop both having graduated from the Philadelphia Textile School, what occured next seemed to follow naturally. Joe Rounsley had already worked out some Indian patterns. He was intrigued with the designs of the Indians and developed a strong feeling for their art. Joe began designing blankets which incorporated the concepts and artistic influences of the American Indian. Always careful to avoid calling them "Indian" blankets, the company offered them as "Indian pattern" blankets. While the Nez Perce connection was helpful, the most important factor was the adoption of the Pendleton blanket by the Indian themselves. These blankets became one measure of the wealth of tribal members, the greater the number of Pendleton "Indian pattern" blankets owned, the wealthier he or she was! They even became for some tribes the required shroud in which a person was buried.

And the white man, too, developed a fondness for the Pendleton "Indian pattern" blanket. Not only for its utility, but for its art as well. Thus, the Indian blanket had two chapters, the one started by the Indians, and the second, the continuation of the design concepts, the expansion of the number of "Indian pattern" blankets available and the extended marketing that was developed by the Pendleton Woolen Mills.

E. W. "Mike" Haggerty
Controller Emeritus
Pendleton Woolen Mills
1929- .

GENERAL CATALOG SHOWING
COLORED ENGRAVINGS

OF

The "Pendleton" Line

MANUFACTURED BY THE

Pendleton Woolen Mills

Pendleton, Oregon

PURE FLEECE WOOL

INDIAN ROBES
BATH ROBES, BED BLANKETS
STEAMER RUGS, COUCH COVERS
TAPESTRIES
SHAWLS

"One of the Comforts of Home"

Pattern No. 501-8

SHOWING DECORATIVE USES OF PENDLETON INDIAN ROBES

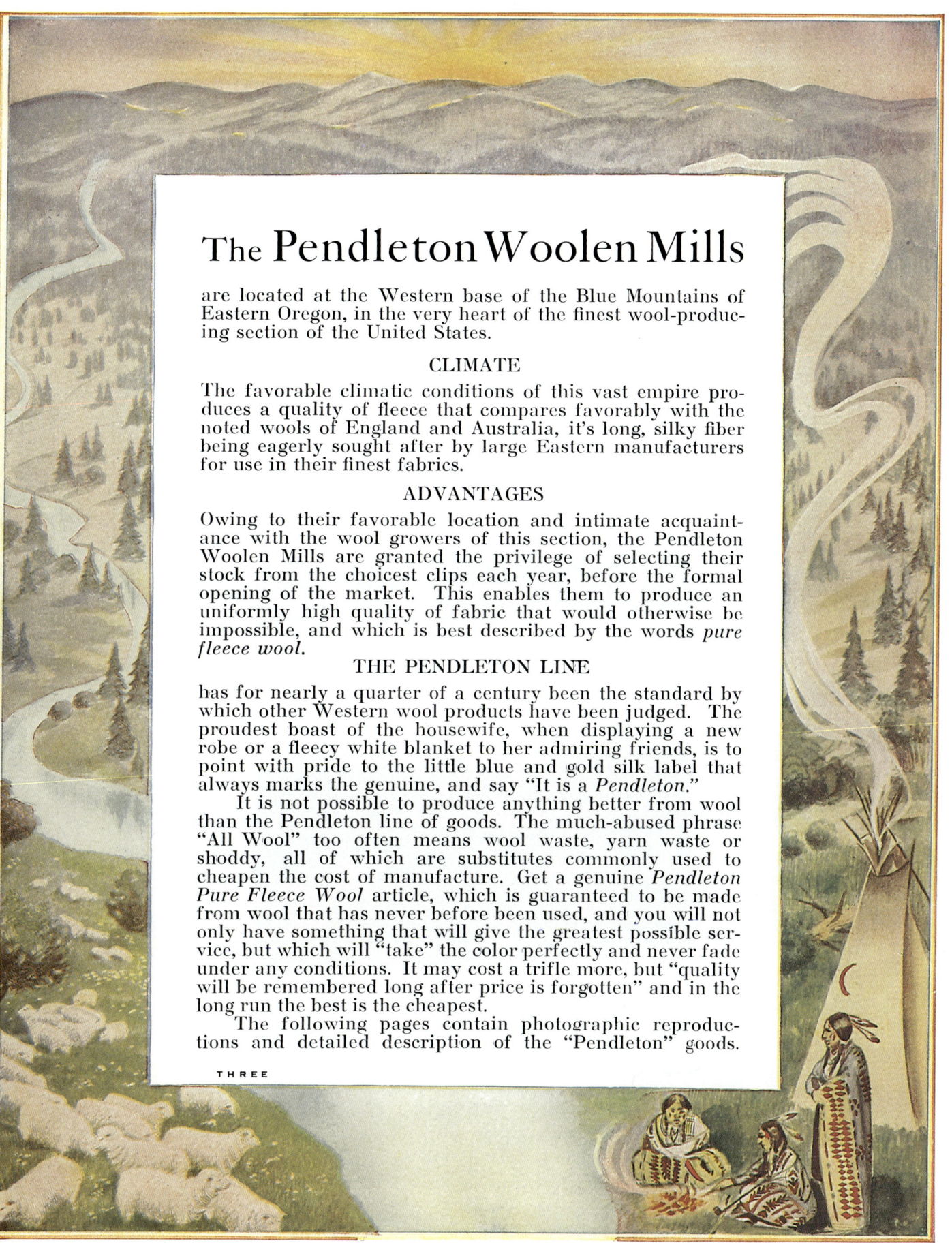

The Pendleton Woolen Mills

are located at the Western base of the Blue Mountains of Eastern Oregon, in the very heart of the finest wool-producing section of the United States.

CLIMATE

The favorable climatic conditions of this vast empire produces a quality of fleece that compares favorably with the noted wools of England and Australia, it's long, silky fiber being eagerly sought after by large Eastern manufacturers for use in their finest fabrics.

ADVANTAGES

Owing to their favorable location and intimate acquaintance with the wool growers of this section, the Pendleton Woolen Mills are granted the privilege of selecting their stock from the choicest clips each year, before the formal opening of the market. This enables them to produce an uniformly high quality of fabric that would otherwise be impossible, and which is best described by the words *pure fleece wool.*

THE PENDLETON LINE

has for nearly a quarter of a century been the standard by which other Western wool products have been judged. The proudest boast of the housewife, when displaying a new robe or a fleecy white blanket to her admiring friends, is to point with pride to the little blue and gold silk label that always marks the genuine, and say "It is a *Pendleton.*"

It is not possible to produce anything better from wool than the Pendleton line of goods. The much-abused phrase "All Wool" too often means wool waste, yarn waste or shoddy, all of which are substitutes commonly used to cheapen the cost of manufacture. Get a genuine *Pendleton Pure Fleece Wool* article, which is guaranteed to be made from wool that has never before been used, and you will not only have something that will give the greatest possible service, but which will "take" the color perfectly and never fade under any conditions. It may cost a trifle more, but "quality will be remembered long after price is forgotten" and in the long run the best is the cheapest.

The following pages contain photographic reproductions and detailed description of the "Pendleton" goods.

THREE

Pendleton Indian Robes

Copyright, Lee Moorehouse, Pendleton, Ore.   Pattern No. 406-2

PURE FLEECE WOOL

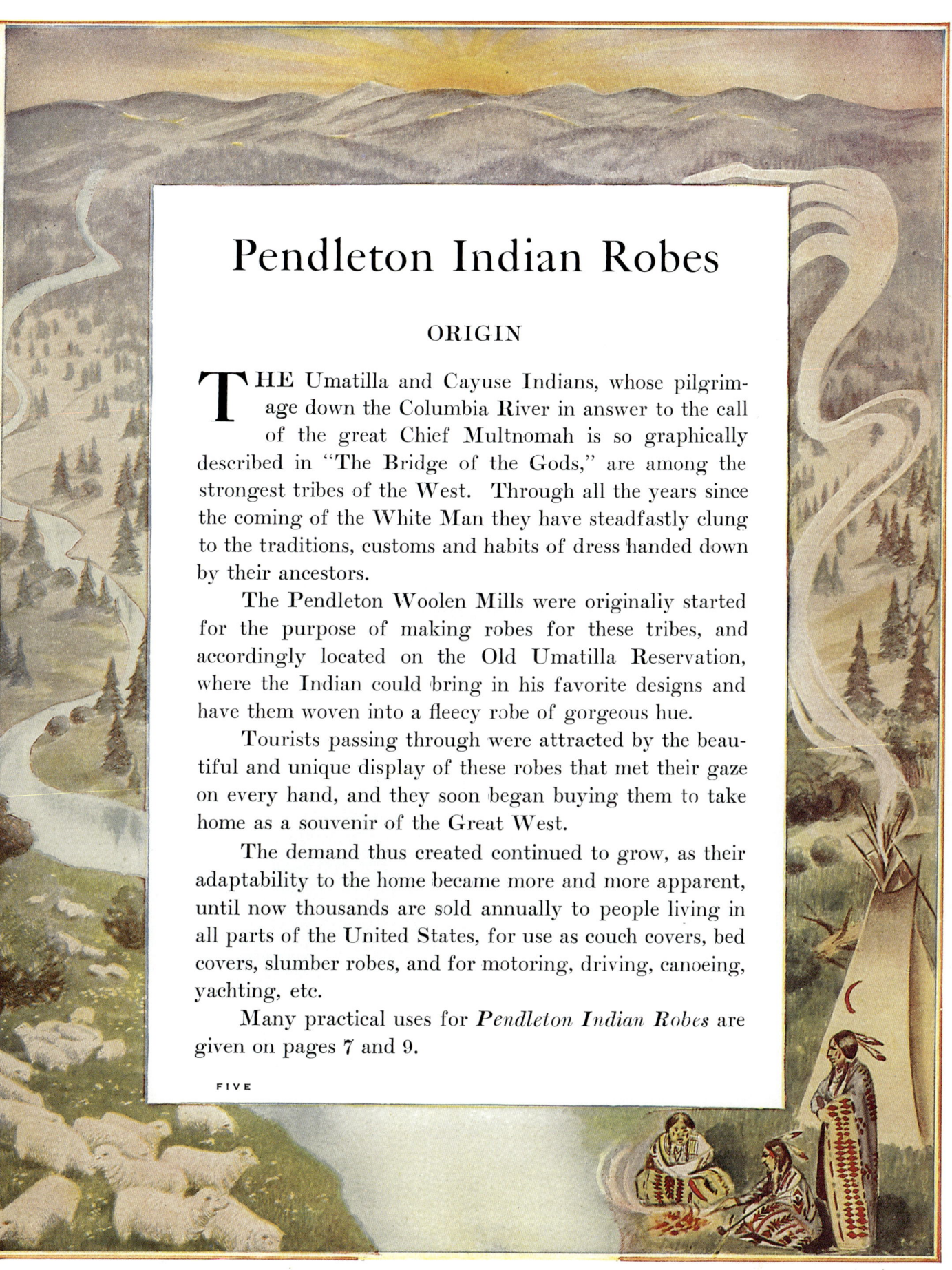

Pendleton Indian Robes

ORIGIN

THE Umatilla and Cayuse Indians, whose pilgrimage down the Columbia River in answer to the call of the great Chief Multnomah is so graphically described in "The Bridge of the Gods," are among the strongest tribes of the West. Through all the years since the coming of the White Man they have steadfastly clung to the traditions, customs and habits of dress handed down by their ancestors.

The Pendleton Woolen Mills were originally started for the purpose of making robes for these tribes, and accordingly located on the Old Umatilla Reservation, where the Indian could bring in his favorite designs and have them woven into a fleecy robe of gorgeous hue.

Tourists passing through were attracted by the beautiful and unique display of these robes that met their gaze on every hand, and they soon began buying them to take home as a souvenir of the Great West.

The demand thus created continued to grow, as their adaptability to the home became more and more apparent, until now thousands are sold annually to people living in all parts of the United States, for use as couch covers, bed covers, slumber robes, and for motoring, driving, canoeing, yachting, etc.

Many practical uses for *Pendleton Indian Robes* are given on pages 7 and 9.

FIVE

No. 28-33

Pendleton Indian Robes

**Price $8.50
Parcel Post Prepaid**

No. 501-26

**PURE
FLEECE
WOOL**

No. 32-5

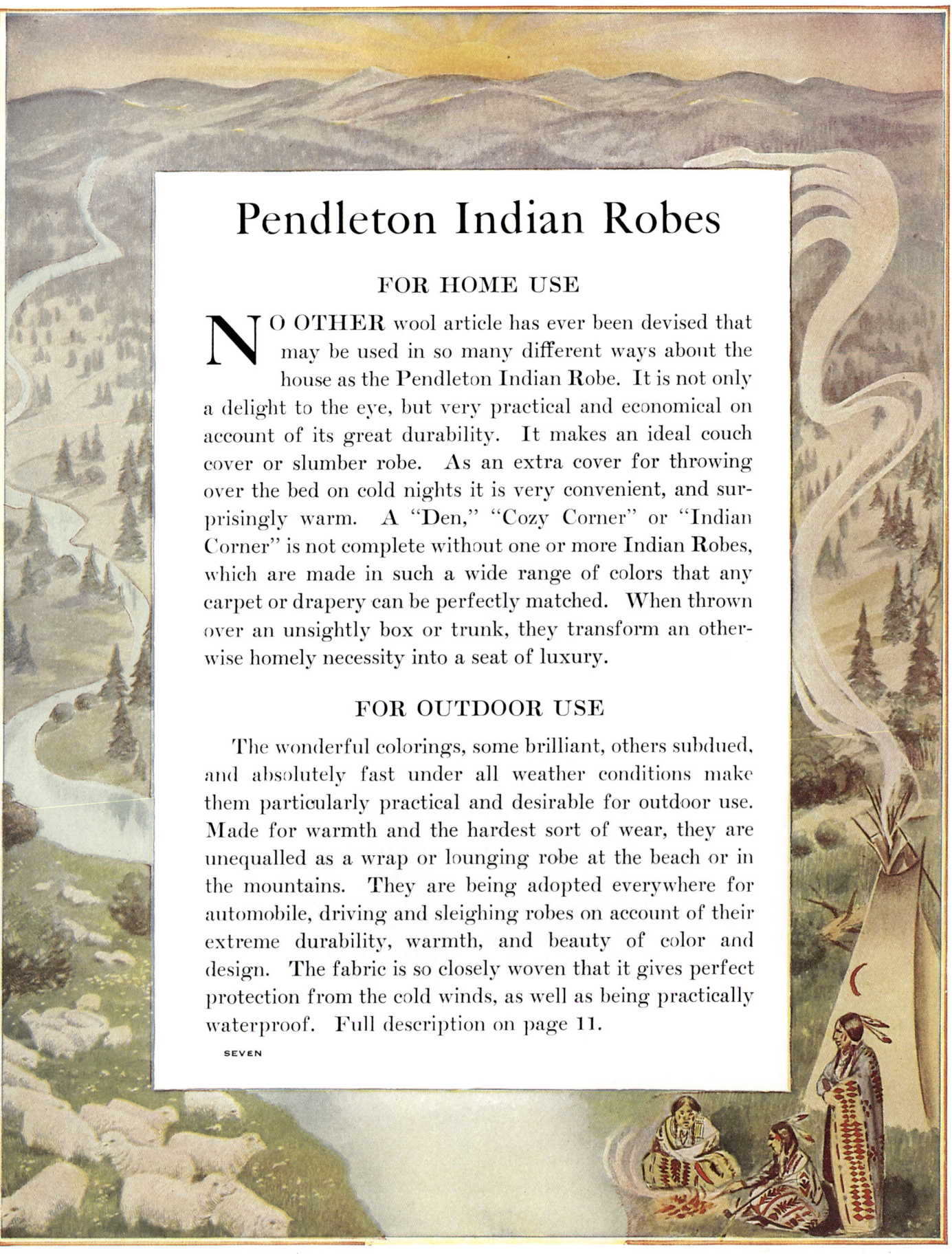

Pendleton Indian Robes

FOR HOME USE

NO OTHER wool article has ever been devised that may be used in so many different ways about the house as the Pendleton Indian Robe. It is not only a delight to the eye, but very practical and economical on account of its great durability. It makes an ideal couch cover or slumber robe. As an extra cover for throwing over the bed on cold nights it is very convenient, and surprisingly warm. A "Den," "Cozy Corner" or "Indian Corner" is not complete without one or more Indian Robes, which are made in such a wide range of colors that any carpet or drapery can be perfectly matched. When thrown over an unsightly box or trunk, they transform an otherwise homely necessity into a seat of luxury.

FOR OUTDOOR USE

The wonderful colorings, some brilliant, others subdued, and absolutely fast under all weather conditions make them particularly practical and desirable for outdoor use. Made for warmth and the hardest sort of wear, they are unequalled as a wrap or lounging robe at the beach or in the mountains. They are being adopted everywhere for automobile, driving and sleighing robes on account of their extreme durability, warmth, and beauty of color and design. The fabric is so closely woven that it gives perfect protection from the cold winds, as well as being practically waterproof. Full description on page 11.

SEVEN

No. 29-31

Pendleton Indian Robes

Price $8.50
Parcel Post Prepaid

No. 27-28

PURE
FLEECE
WOOL

No. 26-30

EIGHT

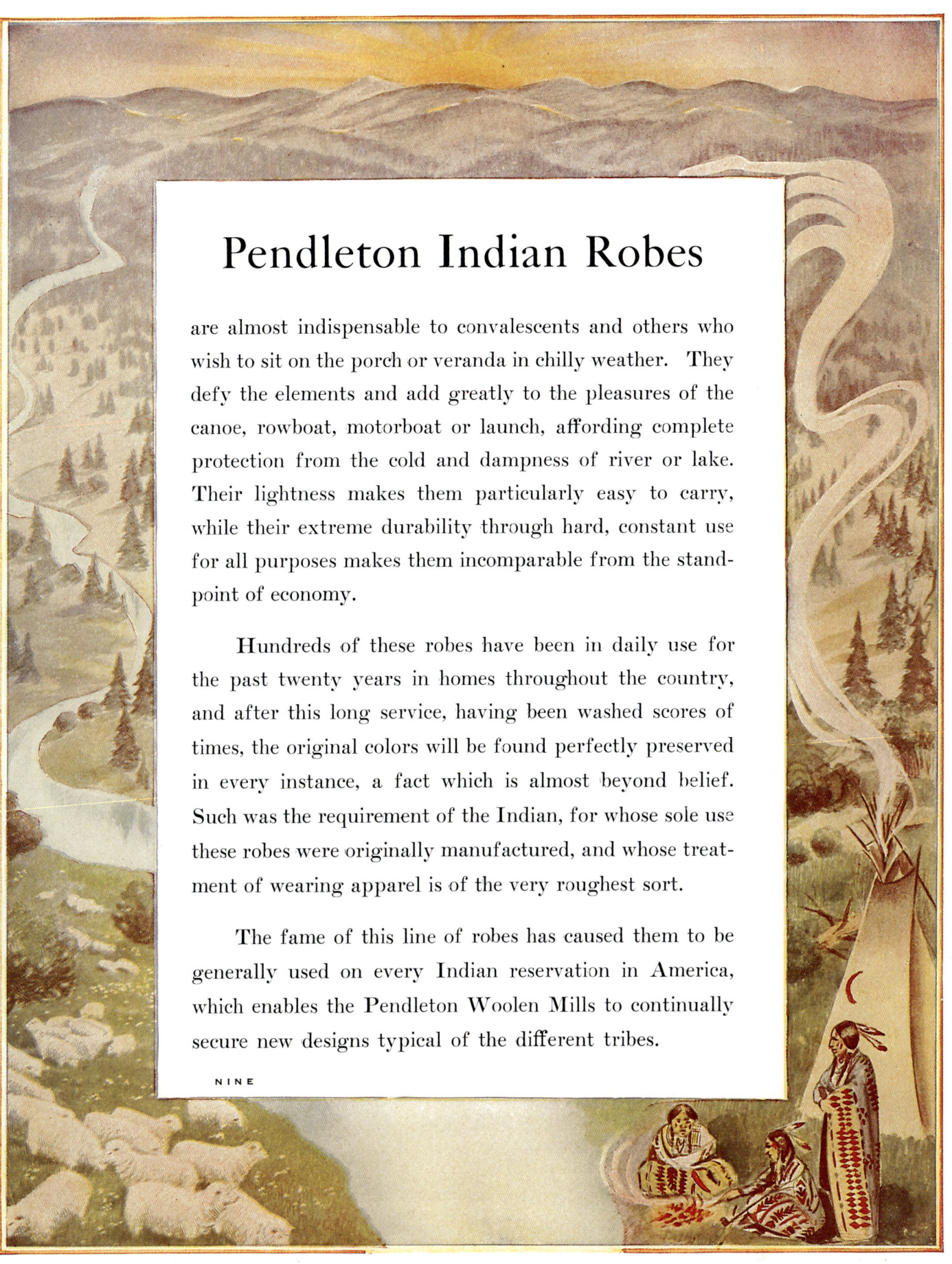

Pendleton Indian Robes

are almost indispensable to convalescents and others who wish to sit on the porch or veranda in chilly weather. They defy the elements and add greatly to the pleasures of the canoe, rowboat, motorboat or launch, affording complete protection from the cold and dampness of river or lake. Their lightness makes them particularly easy to carry, while their extreme durability through hard, constant use for all purposes makes them incomparable from the standpoint of economy.

Hundreds of these robes have been in daily use for the past twenty years in homes throughout the country, and after this long service, having been washed scores of times, the original colors will be found perfectly preserved in every instance, a fact which is almost beyond belief. Such was the requirement of the Indian, for whose sole use these robes were originally manufactured, and whose treatment of wearing apparel is of the very roughest sort.

The fame of this line of robes has caused them to be generally used on every Indian reservation in America, which enables the Pendleton Woolen Mills to continually secure new designs typical of the different tribes.

NINE

No. 531-8

Pendleton
Indian
Robes

Price $8.50
Parcel Post Prepaid

No. 32-4

PURE
FLEECE
WOOL

No. 31-23

TEN

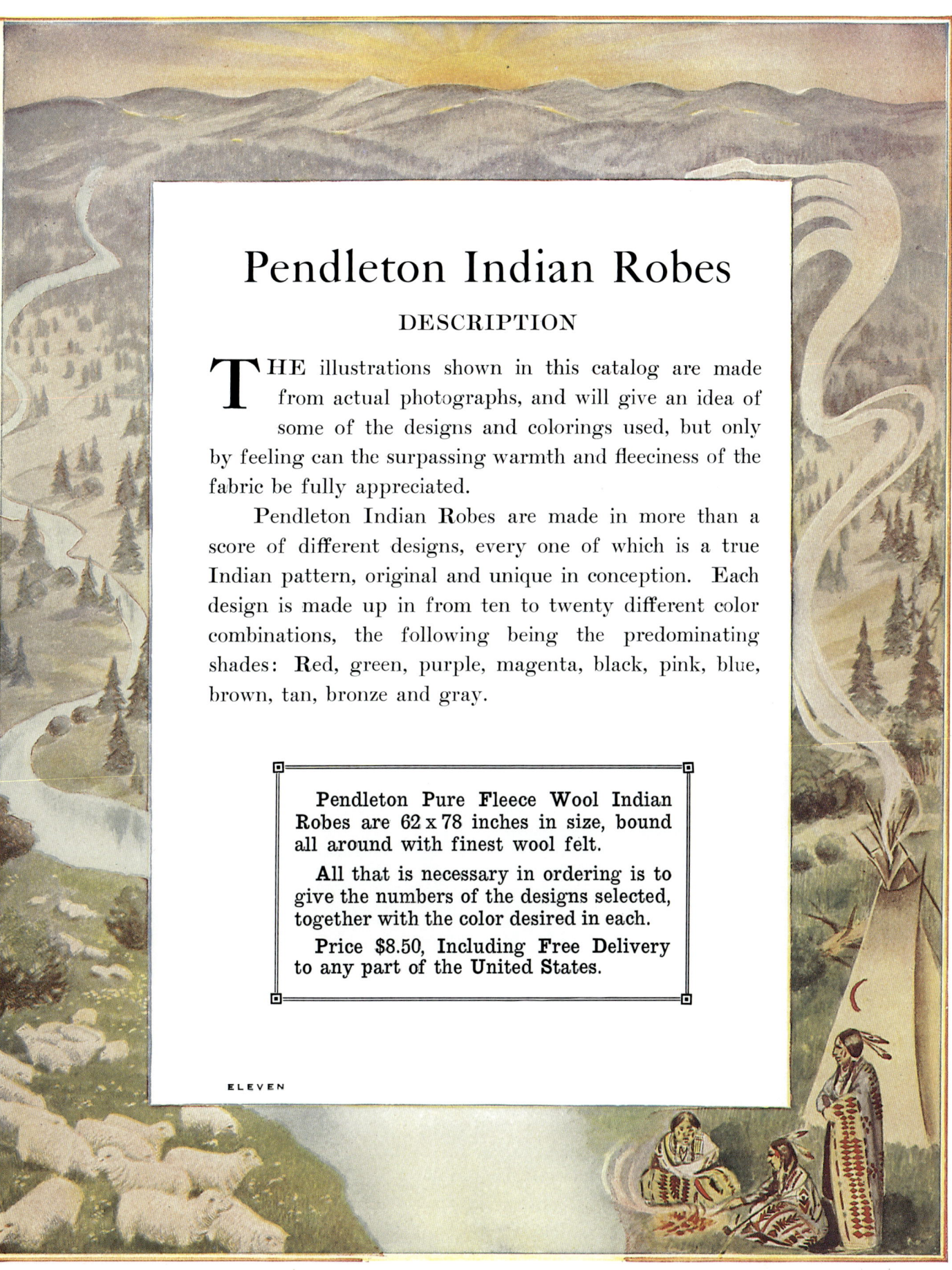

Pendleton Indian Robes

DESCRIPTION

THE illustrations shown in this catalog are made from actual photographs, and will give an idea of some of the designs and colorings used, but only by feeling can the surpassing warmth and fleeciness of the fabric be fully appreciated.

Pendleton Indian Robes are made in more than a score of different designs, every one of which is a true Indian pattern, original and unique in conception. Each design is made up in from ten to twenty different color combinations, the following being the predominating shades: Red, green, purple, magenta, black, pink, blue, brown, tan, bronze and gray.

Pendleton Pure Fleece Wool Indian Robes are 62 x 78 inches in size, bound all around with finest wool felt.

All that is necessary in ordering is to give the numbers of the designs selected, together with the color desired in each.

Price $8.50, Including Free Delivery to any part of the United States.

ELEVEN

PENDLETON INDIAN ROBES—Price $8.50, Parcel Post Prepaid

Pattern No. 522-10

Pattern No. 501-9

Pattern No. 502-5

Pattern No. 503-2

TWELVE

Pendleton Indian Robes

Copyright, Lee Moorehouse, Pendleton, Ore.   Pattern No. 403-4

PURE FLEECE WOOL

PENDLETON INDIAN ROBES—Price $8.50, Parcel Post Prepaid

Pattern No. 705-3

Pattern No. 406-9

Pattern No. 22-7

Pattern No. 403-2

FOURTEEN

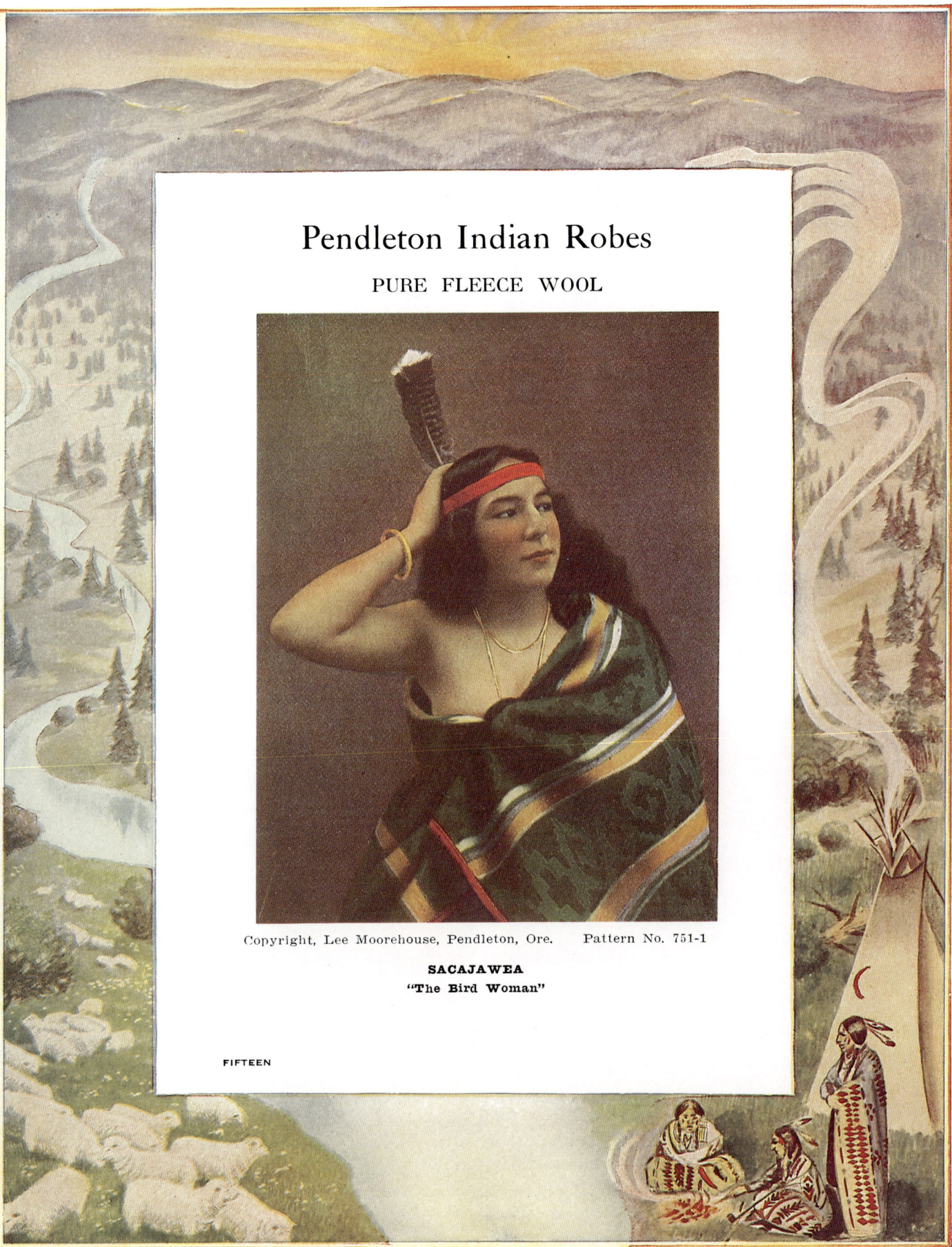

Pendleton Indian Robes

PURE FLEECE WOOL

Copyright, Lee Moorehouse, Pendleton, Ore.   Pattern No. 751-1

SACAJAWEA
"The Bird Woman"

FIFTEEN

PENDLETON INDIAN ROBES—Price $8.50, Parcel Post Prepaid

Pattern No. 404-10

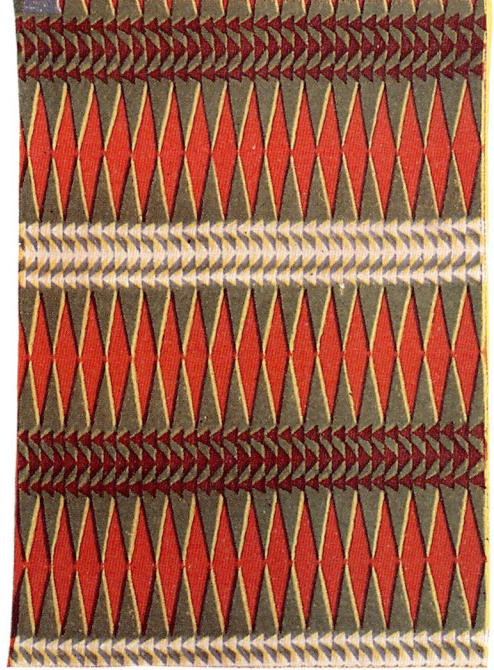

Pattern No. 401-8

Pattern No. 23-7

Pattern No. 531-8

Pendleton Robes are Delightfully
Comfortable for Home Use

Price $8.50   Parcel Post Prepaid

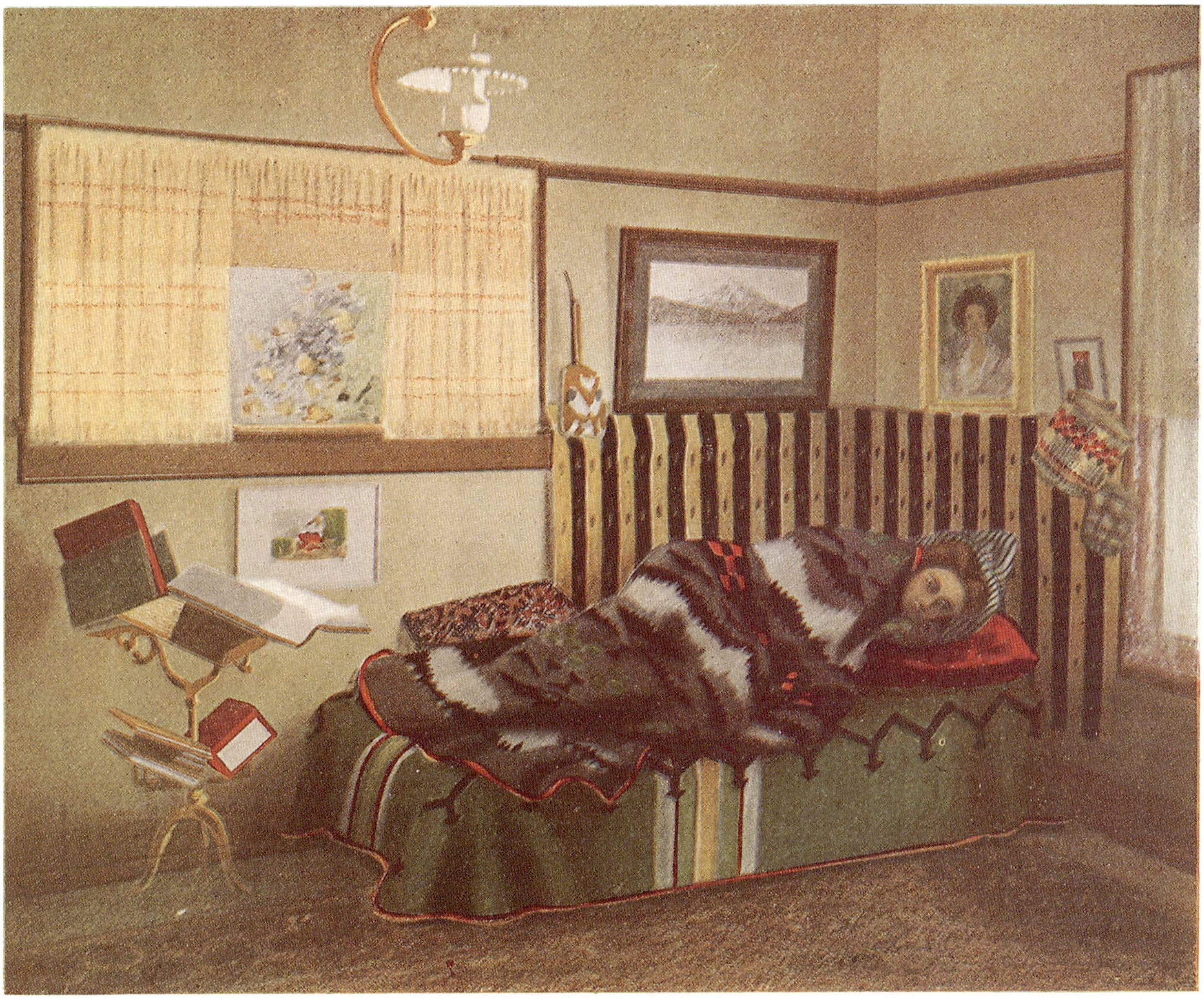

Slumber Robe—Pattern No. 703-5   Indian Robe—Pattern No. 701-4

No BETTER COVERING FOR
THE AFTERNOON NAP

The Original Pendleton Bath Robe

Price $18.50, Parcel Post Prepaid

For additional colors and designs see page 22.

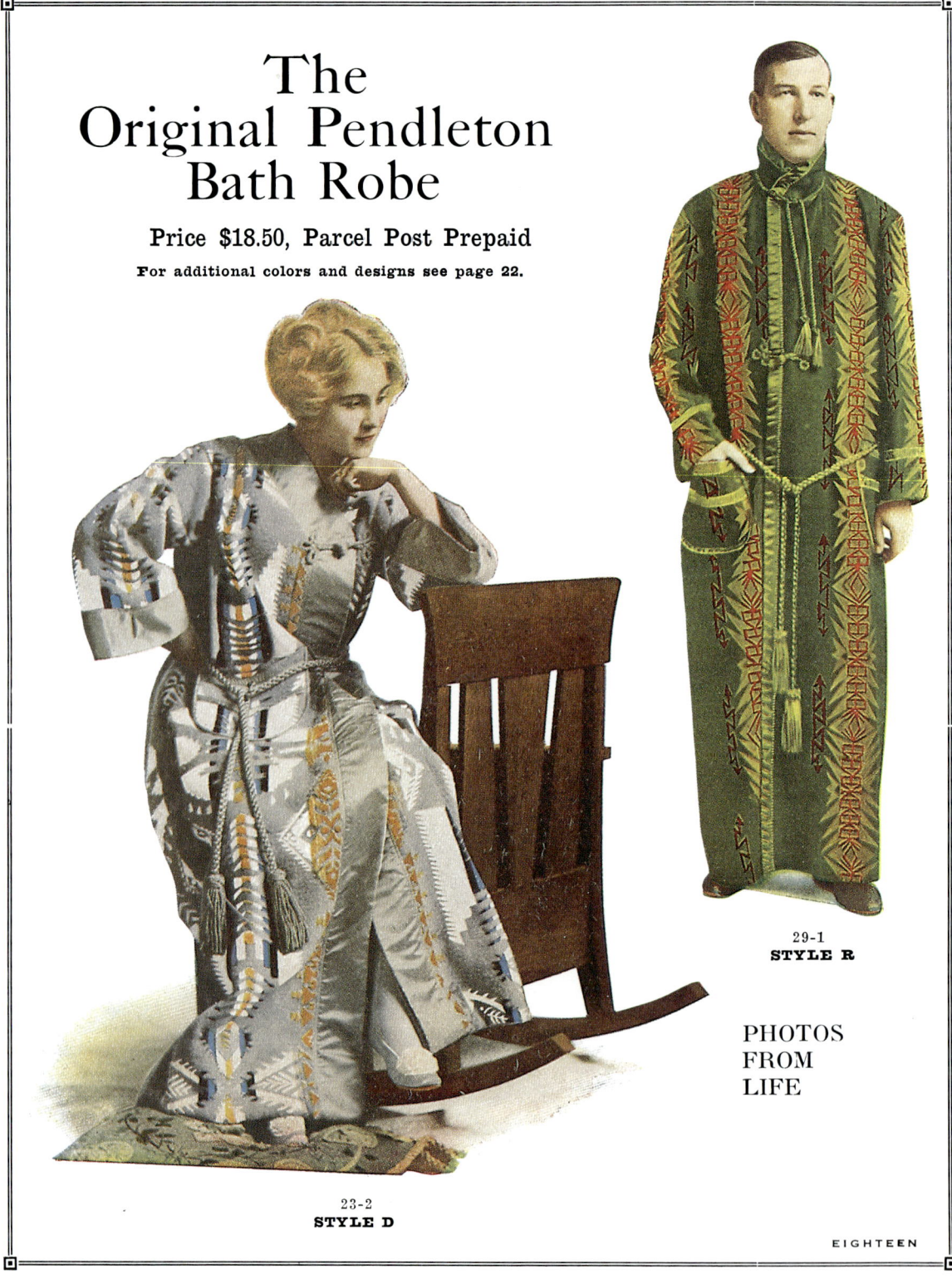

29-1
STYLE R

PHOTOS
FROM
LIFE

23-2
STYLE D

EIGHTEEN

Pendleton Bath Robes

SOMETHING ENTIRELY NEW

THE increasing demand of the white trade for something new and original and yet particularly suggestive of Western Life, has resulted in the introduction of the richest and most beautiful creation in the way of an indoor garment that has ever been manufactured, the *Pendleton Bath Robe,* for men and women.

Adapting the beautiful colorings and designs of the Indian Robe to a garment for general use as a Bath Robe, Lounging Robe or Athletic Robe was such a novel idea that it caused a sensation, resulting in an almost overwhelming demand.

As in the Indian Robes, the fabric is made of the finest Eastern Oregon fleece wool, with a soft velour finish, giving it a warmth and rare fleeciness of feel which appeals to one's love of comfort. A touch reveals their quality, while the beautiful designs and richness of color make them attractive beyond all description.

Price $18.50, Including Free Delivery to any part of the United States

Full descriptions of the various styles will be found on page **23**.

See page **22** for colored illustrations showing additional designs carried in stock.

NINETEEN

PHOTOS
FROM
LIFE

28-3
STYLE C

403-2
STYLE D

The Original Pendleton Bath Robe

Price $18.50 Parcel Post Prepaid

For additional colors and designs see page 22.

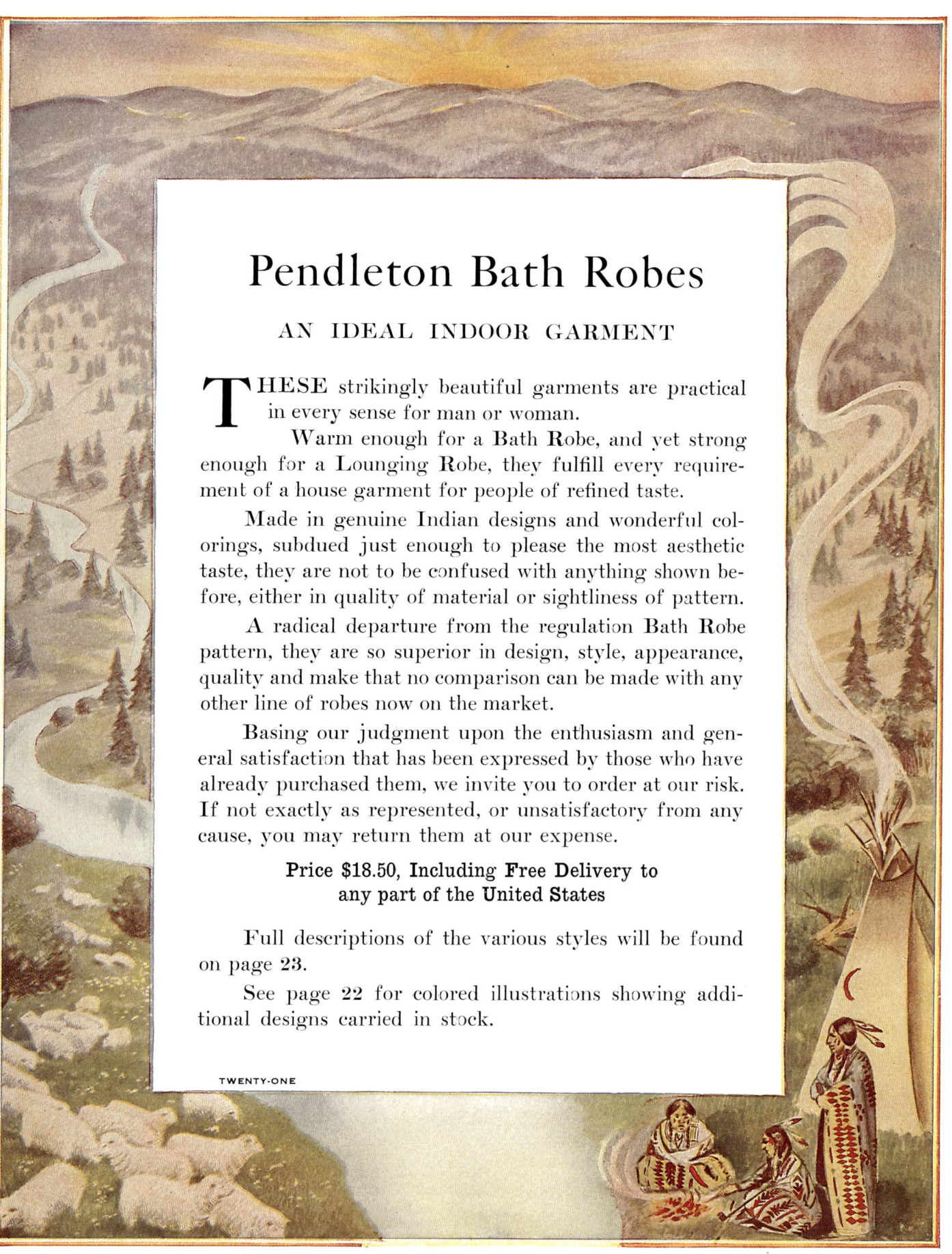

Pendleton Bath Robes

AN IDEAL INDOOR GARMENT

THESE strikingly beautiful garments are practical in every sense for man or woman.

Warm enough for a Bath Robe, and yet strong enough for a Lounging Robe, they fulfill every requirement of a house garment for people of refined taste.

Made in genuine Indian designs and wonderful colorings, subdued just enough to please the most aesthetic taste, they are not to be confused with anything shown before, either in quality of material or sightliness of pattern.

A radical departure from the regulation Bath Robe pattern, they are so superior in design, style, appearance, quality and make that no comparison can be made with any other line of robes now on the market.

Basing our judgment upon the enthusiasm and general satisfaction that has been expressed by those who have already purchased them, we invite you to order at our risk. If not exactly as represented, or unsatisfactory from any cause, you may return them at our expense.

Price $18.50, Including Free Delivery to any part of the United States

Full descriptions of the various styles will be found on page **23**.

See page **22** for colored illustrations showing additional designs carried in stock.

Order
By
Number

Made in
any of the
styles shown
on preceding
pages

The
Original
Pendleton
Bath
Robes

PURE
FLEECE
WOOL

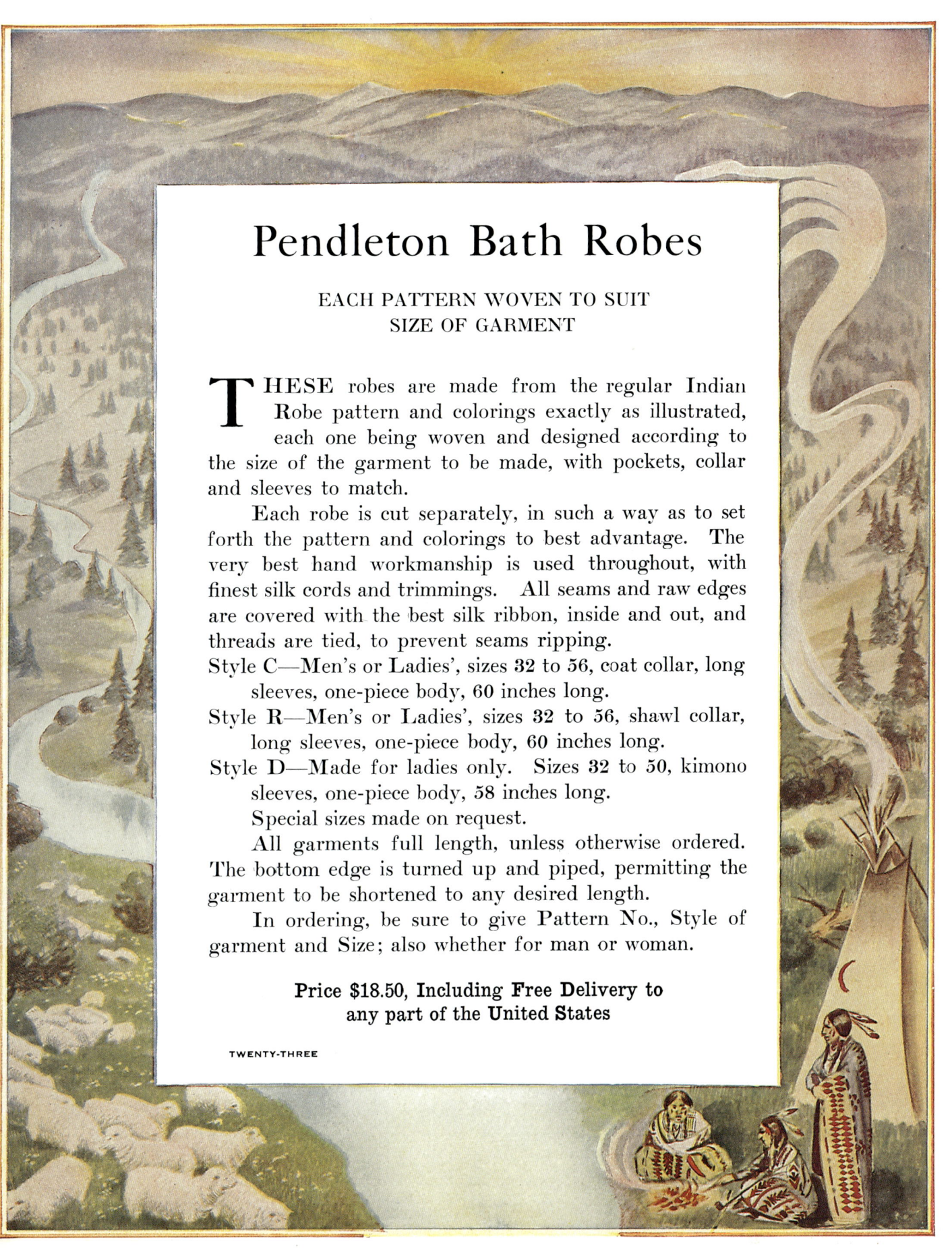

Pendleton Bath Robes

EACH PATTERN WOVEN TO SUIT
SIZE OF GARMENT

THESE robes are made from the regular Indian Robe pattern and colorings exactly as illustrated, each one being woven and designed according to the size of the garment to be made, with pockets, collar and sleeves to match.

Each robe is cut separately, in such a way as to set forth the pattern and colorings to best advantage. The very best hand workmanship is used throughout, with finest silk cords and trimmings. All seams and raw edges are covered with the best silk ribbon, inside and out, and threads are tied, to prevent seams ripping.

Style C—Men's or Ladies', sizes **32** to **56**, coat collar, long sleeves, one-piece body, 60 inches long.

Style R—Men's or Ladies', sizes **32** to **56**, shawl collar, long sleeves, one-piece body, 60 inches long.

Style D—Made for ladies only. Sizes **32** to **50**, kimono sleeves, one-piece body, 58 inches long.

Special sizes made on request.

All garments full length, unless otherwise ordered. The bottom edge is turned up and piped, permitting the garment to be shortened to any desired length.

In ordering, be sure to give Pattern No., Style of garment and Size; also whether for man or woman.

Price $18.50, Including Free Delivery to any part of the United States

Pendleton Couch Covers and Steamer Rugs

**Price $13.00
Parcel
Post
Prepaid**

Pendleton Serape Couch Cover
No. 3

**Price $13.00
Parcel
Post
Prepaid**

Pendleton Couch Cover
No. 27-25

**Price $12.50
Parcel
Post
Prepaid**

PURE
FLEECE
WOOL

Steamer Rug
No. 169-1

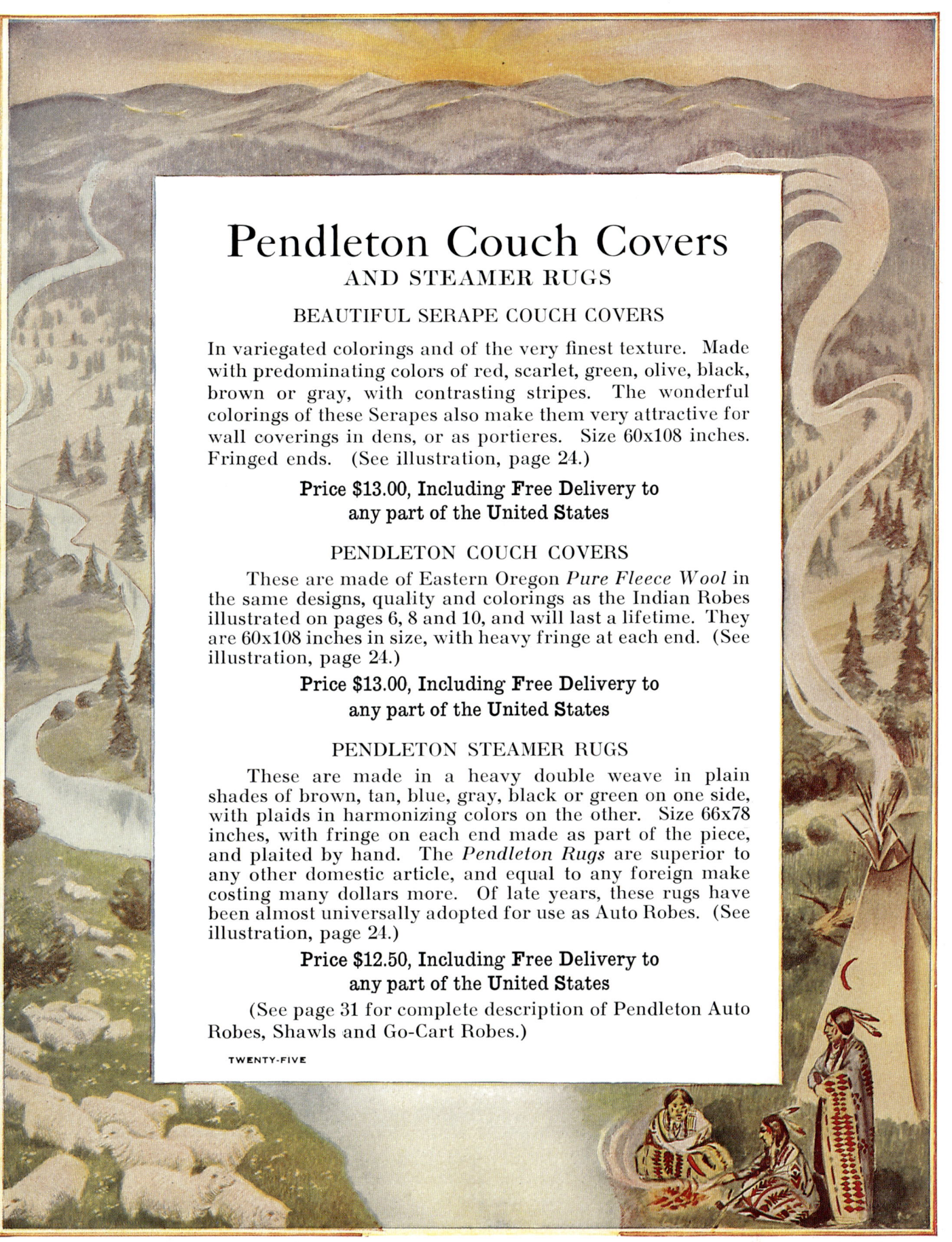

Pendleton Couch Covers
AND STEAMER RUGS

BEAUTIFUL SERAPE COUCH COVERS

In variegated colorings and of the very finest texture. Made with predominating colors of red, scarlet, green, olive, black, brown or gray, with contrasting stripes. The wonderful colorings of these Serapes also make them very attractive for wall coverings in dens, or as portieres. Size 60x108 inches. Fringed ends. (See illustration, page 24.)

Price $13.00, Including Free Delivery to any part of the United States

PENDLETON COUCH COVERS

These are made of Eastern Oregon *Pure Fleece Wool* in the same designs, quality and colorings as the Indian Robes illustrated on pages 6, 8 and 10, and will last a lifetime. They are 60x108 inches in size, with heavy fringe at each end. (See illustration, page 24.)

Price $13.00, Including Free Delivery to any part of the United States

PENDLETON STEAMER RUGS

These are made in a heavy double weave in plain shades of brown, tan, blue, gray, black or green on one side, with plaids in harmonizing colors on the other. Size 66x78 inches, with fringe on each end made as part of the piece, and plaited by hand. The *Pendleton Rugs* are superior to any other domestic article, and equal to any foreign make costing many dollars more. Of late years, these rugs have been almost universally adopted for use as Auto Robes. (See illustration, page 24.)

Price $12.50, Including Free Delivery to any part of the United States

(See page 31 for complete description of Pendleton Auto Robes, Shawls and Go-Cart Robes.)

For complete description see pages 28 and 29.

Pendleton Pure Fleece Wool Bed Blankets

ON the opposite page is a photographic reproduction, in colors, showing some of the Bed Blankets for which the Pendleton Woolen Mills are noted. Superior to all others in appearance, warmth and wearing quality, they are absolutely sanitary on account of being made entirely of new fleece wool.

The immense popularity of Pendleton Bed Blankets demonstrates that there is a constantly growing demand for goods of the highest quality. The public has learned by experience the real economy, satisfaction, pleasure and comfort derived from their use, and we recommend them to the hundreds of thousands of families throughout the land who are able to afford the best, and should not be satisfied with anything else.

On pages 28 and 29 will be found complete descriptions and prices of the various styles shown. All blankets guaranteed exactly as represented.

Pendleton Bed Blankets

PENDLETON FANCY JACQUARD BLANKET. Extra fine.

A—This blanket is made of the very choicest XXXX selected wool. Spun very fine and double woven. Thoroughly fulled and finished with a long thick nap. Especially suitable for guest rooms, and particularly appropriate for wedding and other presents. Woven on a scroll pattern in two colors, white with blue, pink or canary, with finest wide silk binding double stitched with silk thread. Sold either by the pair or in single blankets. Size, 72x90 inches.

Price, including Free Delivery to any part of the United States
Double Blanket $18.00   Single Blanket $9.50

PENDLETON FANCY PLAID BLANKET. Extra fine.

B—The same superior quality of stock and manufacture as in the Fancy Jacquard Blanket described above, excepting in a single weave, with a plaid in two colors, white with blue, pink, lemon or drab. Especially suitable for presents, guest rooms and where it is desirable to have fancy blankets to match other furnishings of a room. Sold either by the pair or in single blankets. Size, 72x84 inches.

Price, including Free Delivery to any part of the United States
Double Blanket $15.00   Single Blanket $8.00

PENDLETON WHITE BLANKET. Extra fine.

C—Made of exactly the same stock and manufacture as the Fancy Jacquard Blanket described above, in the plain white with blue, pink or lemon borders. The superior quality of this blanket makes it especially adapted for general use with the best trade. It is very soft and warm and appeals to people wishing a fine quality blanket in the plain white. This blanket is also made without the colored borders.

Price, including Free Delivery to any part of the United States
Double Blanket—Size 72x84 $12.50   Double Blanket—Size 70x82 $11.50

PENDLETON SANTA ROSA WHITE BLANKET.

D—An all fleece wool blanket made of XXXX wool. Woven wide in the loom, well fulled and finished with a soft thick nap. This blanket is made to supply the demand for a clean sanitary all fleece wool blanket for general use at a popular price. Made with blue or pink borders and bound with silk ribbon stitched with silk thread.

Price, including Free Delivery to any part of the United States
Double Blanket—Size 72x84 $10.00   Double Blanket—Size 70x82 $9.00
Double Blanket—Size 60x90 $10.00   Double Blanket—Size 60x84 $9.00

PENDLETON SAN JOSE WHITE BLANKET.

E—An all XXXX fleece wool filling blanket made on a part cotton warp. This is a fine quality blanket, finished the same as the Santa Rosa described above and well adapted for any indoor purpose.

Price, including Free Delivery to any part of the United States
Double Blanket—Size 72x84 $9.00   Double Blanket—Size 70x82 $8.00
Double Blanket—Size 60x90 $9.00   Double Blanket—Size 64x84 $8.00

PENDLETON ANGELES FAWN BLANKET.

F—A beautiful all fleece wool filling blanket in a light tan color with a border to match. This blanket is made the same as the San Jose described above, on a cotton warp and is one of the most sightly and serviceable in the line. The color makes it well adapted for either indoor or outdoor purpose. Bound with a cream silk binding and stitched with silk thread.

Price, including Free Delivery to any part of the United States
Double Blanket—Size 72x84 $8.50   Double Blanket—Size 70x82 $7.50

PENDLETON ANGELES SILVER GRAY BLANKET.

G—Same as the Fawn described above, the only difference being in the color, which is a very beautiful light shade of gray, with border of white and blue.

Price, including Free Delivery to any part of the United States
Double Blanket—Size 72x84 $8.50   Double Blanket—Size 70x82 $7.50

Pendleton Bed Blankets

H—PENDLETON GRAY BLANKET

THIS blanket is made to supply a demand for something equally as fine in quality as the best grade of white blanket, and has the advantage of being less easily soiled, making it particularly desirable for general home use. Silver gray in color, with four-inch silk binding. A very fine article, and one of our largest sellers.

Price, including Free Delivery to any part of the United States

Double Blanket—Size 70x90 . . . . $15.00
Double Blanket—Size 74x86 . . . . 12.50
Double Blanket—Size 72x84 . . . . 10.00
Double Blanket—Size 70x82 . . . . 8.50

PENDLETON VICUNA, MOTTLE AND SCARLET BLANKETS
PRICES SAME AS ABOVE

Made in the same fleece wool quality and same sizes as the Gray Blanket described above. These colored blankets are similar in general appearance to the Umatilla Blankets I, J and K, illustrated on page 26.

The Vicuna is a blanket particularly adapted for the general use of stockmen, miners, surveyors, logging men and others who are not so situated as to properly care for a white or light colored article.

The Mottle, or double and twist blanket, was originally made for the Alaska trade, and is the most durable blanket on the market. It is made of a black and white yarn twisted together, which produces the mottled effect.

The Scarlet is believed by many people to be the warmest and most sanitary blanket made. Colors guaranteed fast.

L—PENDLETON ARMY BLANKET

Regulation olive drab color, made single or double, and in sizes suitable for either a single or double bed. This is a blanket particularly adapted for camping and general outdoor purposes, and should be found in every outfit.

Price, including Free Delivery to any part of the United States

Double Blanket—Size 72x84 . . . . $15.00
Double Blanket—Size 64x84 . . . . 12.50
Double Blanket—Size 60x80 . . . . 10.00

PENDLETON HUDSON BAY BLANKETS

These are true copies of the blankets that were introduced among the Indians by the early traders, and are made in red, blue, white, green, gray, purple, black, and magenta, with a four-inch black stripe at each end. They are also marked with different length black "points" woven in the edge to designate the size and weight without which the Indian would not have them. They are made without binding.

Price, including Free Delivery to any part of the United States

Double Blanket—Size 64x80 . . . . $8.00
Double Blanket—Size 60x80 . . . . 7.00
Double Blanket—Size 56x78 . . . . 6.00

Umatilla and Yakima Bed Blankets

THESE two lines of blankets are manufactured to supply a class of trade that requires warmth and durability in a wool blanket for practical use, and yet cannot afford to purchase the finest fleece wool goods. They represent the very best values that it is possible to produce at the price asked, and are not to be classed with the ordinary trade blanket made from a mixture of cotton and shoddy, with very little if any new wool used.

They will be found entirely satisfactory in every respect, and will wash perfectly.

UMATILLA VICUNA (I), TIGER MOTTLE (J), AND SCARLET (K) BLANKETS

Are illustrated on page 26. We also make a very nice gray blanket in this quality, in a medium light shade.

Price, including Free Delivery to any part of the United States

Double Blanket—Size 72x86 . . . . $11.00
Double Blanket—Size 70x82 . . . . 9.00
Double Blanket—Size 70x80 . . . . 8.00

YAKIMA MOTTLE AND VICUNA BLANKETS

Are not illustrated. They are made from coarser stock than the Umatilla grade, and are ideal blankets for common use, especially for outdoor purposes. Similar in color to J and I shown in the Umatilla line, but with slightly different borders, and instead of being bound, the edges are woven in a contrasting color, then turned back and stitched, making a very durable finish.

Price, including Free Delivery to any part of the United States

Double Blanket—Size 72x86 . . . . $8.50
Double Blanket—Size 70x82 . . . . 7.50
Double Blanket—Size 64x80 . . . . 6.50
Double Blanket—Size 60x80 . . . . 5.50
Double Blanket—Size 56x72 . . . . 4.50

YAKIMA GRAY BLANKETS

Similar to above, only made in a dark gray mix and well adapted for hard usage.

Price, including Free Delivery to any part of the United States

Double Blanket—Size 72x84 . . . . $8.00
Double Blanket—Size 70x84 . . . . 7.00
Double Blanket—Size 64x80 . . . . 6.00
Double Blanket—Size 60x80 . . . . 5.00
Double Blanket—Size 56x72 . . . . 4.00

Pendleton Auto Robes

IN INDIAN DESIGNS

FOR those who prefer something larger and heavier than the regular Indian Robe as described and illustrated on pages 4 to 17, we have made a special robe for automobile use that is very desirable. Made in any of the Indian patterns and colorings as illustrated, 68x86 inches in size, it is preferred by many to the regulation Auto or Steamer Robe with fringed ends, on account of its unique and attractive appearance.

Price, including **Free Delivery** to any part of the United States $12.50

PENDLETON INDIAN SHAWLS

These are in the same patterns and colors as the Indian Robes illustrated, and are fringed all around, making a very attractive and sightly wrap. Size, 62x66 inches.

Price, including **Free Delivery** to any part of the United States $10.00

PENDLETON SERAPE SHAWLS

Made in the same patterns and colorings as the couch covers illustrated and described on pages 24 and 25. Hard woven, without napping, giving them a worsted or cashmere finish. Size, 62x66 inches.

Price, including **Free Delivery** to any part of the United States $10.00

PENDLETON PLAIN AND PLAID SHAWLS

These are in lighter weights than the regular Pendleton Indian Shawls described above, and come in gray, black, brown, red, green, blue, purple, magenta, pink and white colors. Two weights, 1½ lb. and 2 lb. Size, 64x64.

Price, including **Free Delivery** to any part of the United States, 1½ lb......................$4.00
2   lb....................... 5.00

PENDLETON GO-CART ROBES

These "Muchacho" or papoose robes are in the same quality, patterns and colors as the regular Indian Robes, only being in a size adapted for use in the go-cart, for which they are very practical. They will not require washing nearly so often as any other kind of robe. Size, 32x40.

Price, including **Free Delivery** to any part of the United States $2.50

YAKIMA INDIAN ROBES

Made in the same weight and size as the Pendleton Robes, only of coarser stock, and in plainer designs.

Price, including **Free Delivery** to any part of the United States $7.00

MOKI INDIAN ROBES

A smaller and lighter robe than the Yakima. Size, 60x72.

Price, including **Free Delivery** to any part of the United States $5.50

CAYUSE INDIAN ROBES

Same size as the Moki, but lighter in weight, and less closely woven. A very satisfactory, cheap robe.

Price, including **Free Delivery** to any part of the United States $4.50

Organization & Equipment

AFTER looking through this catalog you have doubtless concluded that it is out of the ordinary. It describes and illustrates an *extraordinary* line of goods. In fact, there is no line of woolen goods manufactured by any other mill that is so unique in many respects as the *Pendleton Line,* nor is there another mill that is so splendidly equipped for specializing in this class of goods as the *Pendleton Woolen Mills.*

Favored as they are by location and environment, they not only have every machine of worth that is known to the modern textile industry, but the different departments are all in the hands of men who have spent years in the study of their particular lines of work, and the combined product of their hands and brains is as nearly perfect as it is possible to achieve.

THIS BLUE AND GOLD LABEL

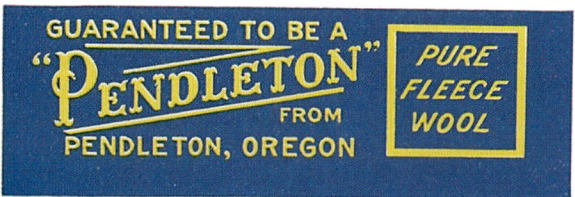

stands for twenty years of honest, intelligent effort directed towards the production of strictly high-class *Fleece Wool Goods,* and is an absolute guarantee of quality. It is the mark of the genuine, and will be found on every *Pendleton Blanket or Robe, the Best Made.*

Pendleton Woolen Mills
Pendleton, Oregon

Other Titles Available

Mesa Verde Ancient Architecture by Jesse Walter Fewkes, Introduction by Larry V. Nordby. Essays on the archaeological and architectural finds at the Cliff Palace and Spruce Tree House. The Introduction is a current update on the contemporary research being done at these sites by the National Park's chief research archaeologist. 216 pages; PB; Price $16.95.

Kachinas, Spirit Beings of the Hopi Paintings by Neil David Sr., Descriptions by J. Brent Ricks and Alexander Anthony. Based on 79 paintings by Hopi artist and Kachina carver Neil David Sr., that depict rare Kachinas and deities of the Hopi Indians. 200 pages; HB; Price $50.00.

Heart of the Dragonfly by Allison Bird. The book, discussing the development and historyof the cross necklaces of the Pueblo and Navajo Indians, is filled with historic photographs showing Indians wearing cross necklaces in social and ceremonial settings. 208 pages; PB; Price $39.95.

Moki Snake Dance by Walter Hough PhD, Introduction by Joseph Traugott. This travel guide originally published by the Santa Fe Railroad in 1899 describes the unparalleled drama of the Snake Dance ceremonial of the Moki (Hopi) Indians of Arizona. 80 pages; 75 b/w photos; PB; Price $5.95.

The Mimbres, Art and Archaeology by Jesse Walter Fewkes; Introduction by J.J. Brody. The insightful overview provided by noted Mimbres authority, J.J. Brody, introduces the original research and writings done between 1914 and 1934 by noted ethnographer, J.W. Fewkes. 182 pages; PB; 300+ illustrations; Price $16.95.

Zuni Fetishism by Ruth Kirk. The story of the Fetishes used in Zuni religion and ceremony. 72 pages; PB; Price $4.75.

ORDER(S) MAY BE SENT TO:
AVANYU PUBLISHING, INC.
PO BOX 27134
ALBUQUERQUE, NM 87125
TELEPHONE 505 341 1280 OR
E-MAIL AT BRENTRIC@AOL.COM.